Real-life maths

This book belongs to

....

Colour the star when you complete a page.
See how far you've come!

Author: Sarah-Anne Fernandes

How to use this book

- This book takes a thematic approach to real-world maths to engage your child with maths that they can recognise in their everyday life.
- Find a quiet, comfortable place to work, away from distractions.
- Make sure your child has some paper to write their ideas and workings on.
- Help with reading the instructions where necessary and ensure that your child understands what to do.
- Within each theme there are lots of problem-solving and reasoning activities for your child to complete. Your child will have to select and apply the appropriate number, measurement, geometry and/or statistics skills to solve each problem.
- Always end each activity before your child gets tired so that they will be eager to return next time.
- Help and encourage your child to check their own answers as they complete each activity.
- Let your child return to their favourite pages once they have been completed. Talk about the activities they enjoyed and what they have learnt.
- Reward your child with plenty of praise and encouragement.

Special features of this book:

- **Progress chart:** when your child has completed a page, ask them to colour in the relevant star on the first page of the book. This will enable you to keep track of progress through the activities and help to motivate your child.
- **Learning tip:** situated in a yellow box at the bottom of the page, this offers further guidance, suggests further activities and encourages discussion about what your child has learnt.

Published by Collins
An imprint of HarperCollins*Publishers* Ltd
The News Building
1 London Bridge Street
London SE1 9GF

HarperCollins*Publishers*
Macken House, 39/40 Mayor Street Upper,
Dublin 1, D01 C9W8, Ireland

© HarperCollins*Publishers* Ltd 2026

10 9 8 7 6 5 4 3 2 1

ISBN 978-0-00-877530-8

The author asserts the moral right to be identified as the author of this work.

All rights reserved. No part of this publication may be reproduced, stored in a retrieval system, or transmitted, in any form or by any means, electronic, mechanical, photocopying, recording or otherwise, without the prior permission of Collins.

Without limiting the exclusive rights of any author, contributor or the publisher of this publication, any unauthorised use of this publication to train generative artificial intelligence (AI) technologies is expressly prohibited. HarperCollins also exercise their rights under Article 4(3) of the Digital Single Market Directive 2019/790 and expressly reserve this publication from the text and data mining exception.

British Library Cataloguing in Publication Data

A Catalogue record for this publication is available from the British Library.

Author: Sarah-Anne Fernandes
Publisher: Fiona McGlade
Editor: Katie Galloway
Cover design: Sarah Duxbury and Amparo Barrera
Interior concept design: Ian Wrigley
Page layouts: QBS Learning and Ian Wrigley
Production: Bethany Brohm
All images © Shutterstock.com and © HarperCollins*Publishers*
Printed in the UK

Contents

At the supermarket	4
Around the world	8
At the post office	12
At the garden centre	16
Bake off!	20
Looking after the planet	24
Visiting a castle	26
At the leisure centre	30
Answers	32

At the supermarket

You are shopping at the supermarket. Look at weights of foods, how prices add up on receipts and ways to save money.

1 At the supermarket, you, Dad and Flo each choose one meal deal.

You choose the stir-fry meal deal for **£4**

Find the total cost of all the individual items.

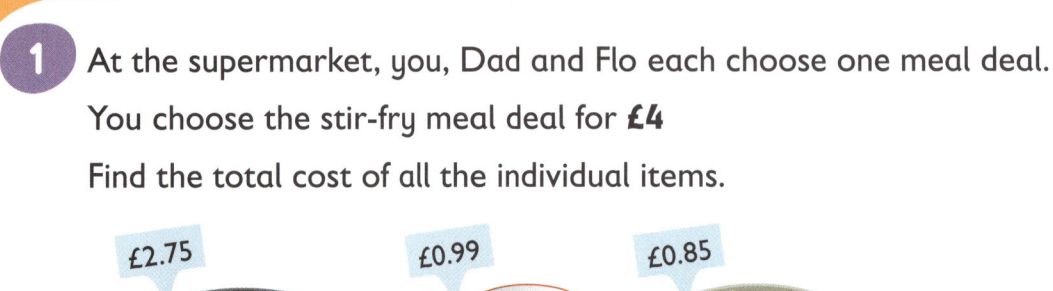

£ ☐

How much money do you save on the meal deal?   ☐ p

Dad chooses the curry meal deal for **£6**

Find the total cost of all the individual items.

£ ☐

How much money does Dad save on the meal deal?   ☐ p

Flo chooses the pizza meal deal for **£5**

Find the total cost of all the individual items.

£ ☐

How much money does Flo save on the meal deal?   ☐ p

Your child needs to understand that 'savings' means the amount of money you have not spent. When adding 99p, it is beneficial to show your child that it is easier to round 99p up to £1 then add the £1 and take away 1p.

2 Jin is in the fruit section. Jin weighs these fruits on the digital scales.
Write the mass of each fruit in **grams**.

☐ g ☐ g ☐ g

Bananas cost 90p per kilo.

What is the cost of the bananas Jin has weighed on the scale? £ ☐

Apples cost 30p per quarter kilo.

What is the cost of the apples Jin has weighed on the scale? ☐ p

3 Supermarket parking is free for 1 hour 30 minutes. After this, shoppers must pay £1.10 per hour.

Charlie arrives at the supermarket car park at 10.45 am and leaves at 11.30 am.

Circle the cost of his parking ticket.

Bindi arrives at the supermarket car park at 12.35 pm and leaves at 3 pm.

Circle the cost of her parking ticket.

Sara arrives at the supermarket car park at 6.05 pm and leaves at 18:55.

Circle the cost of her parking ticket.

4 Fran, Kodie and Alex each have a supermarket points card. Points add up to discount vouchers.

Fran has **750 points**. She needs **180 more points** to get a discount voucher.

How many points does Fran need in total to get the discount voucher?

Kodie has **378 points**. He needs **500** points in total to get a discount voucher.

How many more points does Kodie need to get the discount voucher?

Alex has **1000 points**. He only needs **850 points** to get a discount voucher.

How many points will Alex have left on his card after getting the voucher?

5 Fran, Kodie and Alex use their discount vouchers on their shopping bills.

What do they each pay?

Fran
RECEIPT
TOTAL
£11.75
discount voucher
£1.50

Kodie
RECEIPT
TOTAL
£23.80
discount voucher
£2.50

Alex
RECEIPT
TOTAL
£48.90
discount voucher
£5.00

£ ☐   £ ☐   £ ☐

6 The pictogram shows the number of sandwiches sent to the local food bank from different supermarkets.

🥪 = 50 sandwiches	
Supermarket A	🥪 🥪 🥪
Supermarket B	🥪 🥪 🥪 🥪 🥪
Supermarket C	🥪 🥪

How many sandwiches are sent to the food bank from Supermarket A?

How many more sandwiches are sent from Supermarket B than from Supermarket C?

How many sandwiches are sent to the food bank in total?

7 The supermarket gets a delivery of 90 crates.
Each crate has 100 boxes.

How many boxes are delivered?

Half of the boxes contain tins that need to be unpacked.

1000 tins are unpacked in the morning.

How many more tins need to be unpacked in the afternoon?

Your child needs to understand how to multiply and divide a one-digit or two-digit number by 10 and 100 and explain the effect on the place value of the digit. For example:
- If we multiply by 10, each digit moves one place to the left: 78 × 10 = 780
- If we multiply by 100, each digit moves two places to the left: 78 × 100 = 7800
- When we divide by 10 or 100, the digits move to the right.

Around the world

There are many countries to learn about, with different geographical features, weather, currency and time zones.

1 The table shows the approximate length of different rivers.

Nile	Congo	Amazon	Mississippi
6650 km	4700 km	6400 km	3766 km

Put the rivers in order from **shortest** to **longest**.

_____ _____ _____ _____

Calculate the difference between the length of the Nile and the length of the Mississippi. ☐ km

The Yangtze is 100 km shorter than the Amazon. What is the length of the Yangtze? ☐ km

2 Draw lines to match the cities' temperatures with the thermometers.

| London 15°C | Reykjavik 7°C | Madrid 21°C | Rome 28°C |

Your child needs to know how to order and compare numbers by identifying the place value of each digit in a number. Roll a dice three or four times each to generate 3-digit and 4-digit numbers and decide who wins by identifying who has rolled the largest number.

3 Different countries use different currencies. In much of Europe, the currency is the euro (€).

Exchange the amounts into **euros** and **cents** using the exchange rate of £1 = 1 euro and 20 cents (€1.20).

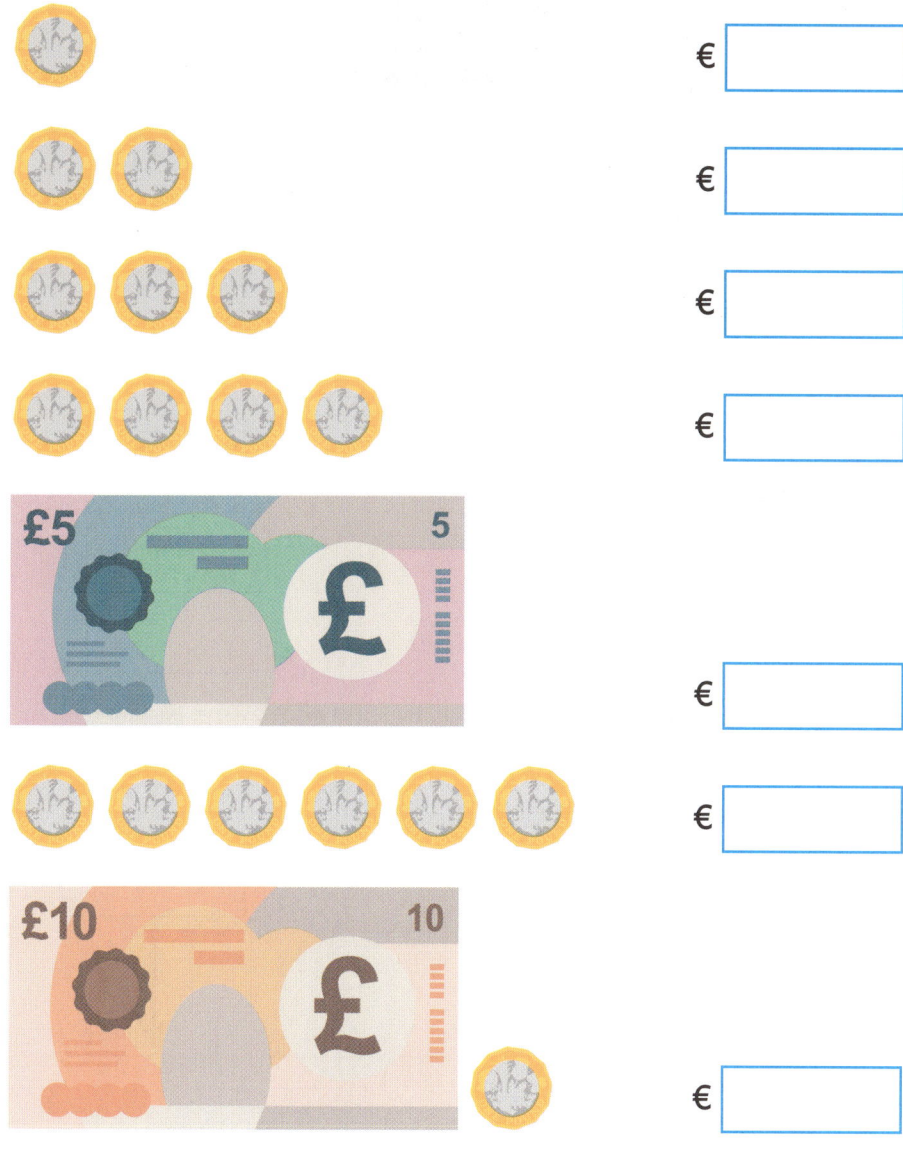

€ ☐

€ ☐

€ ☐

€ ☐

€ ☐

€ ☐

€ ☐

Your child needs to recognise coins and notes to find the total amount. To convert money, such as from pounds to euros, they need to have knowledge of simple scaling, for example:
- £1 is approximately equal to 1 euro 20 cents
- £2 is approximately equal to 2 euros 40 cents.

4 Different parts of the world have different time zones.

Millie is in London in England. The time in London is shown on this 24-hour clock:

Write the 24-hour time for each city.

New York is **5 hours behind** London. ☐ : ☐

Moscow is **2 hours ahead** of London. ☐ : ☐

Tokyo is **8 hours ahead** of London. ☐ : ☐

Delhi is $4\frac{1}{2}$ **hours ahead** of London. ☐ : ☐

Calgary is **7 hours behind** London. ☐ : ☐

Wellington is **12 hours ahead** of London. ☐ : ☐

5 The number line shows the approximate height of Mount Everest, the highest mountain in the world.

Write the height of Mount Everest in the box.

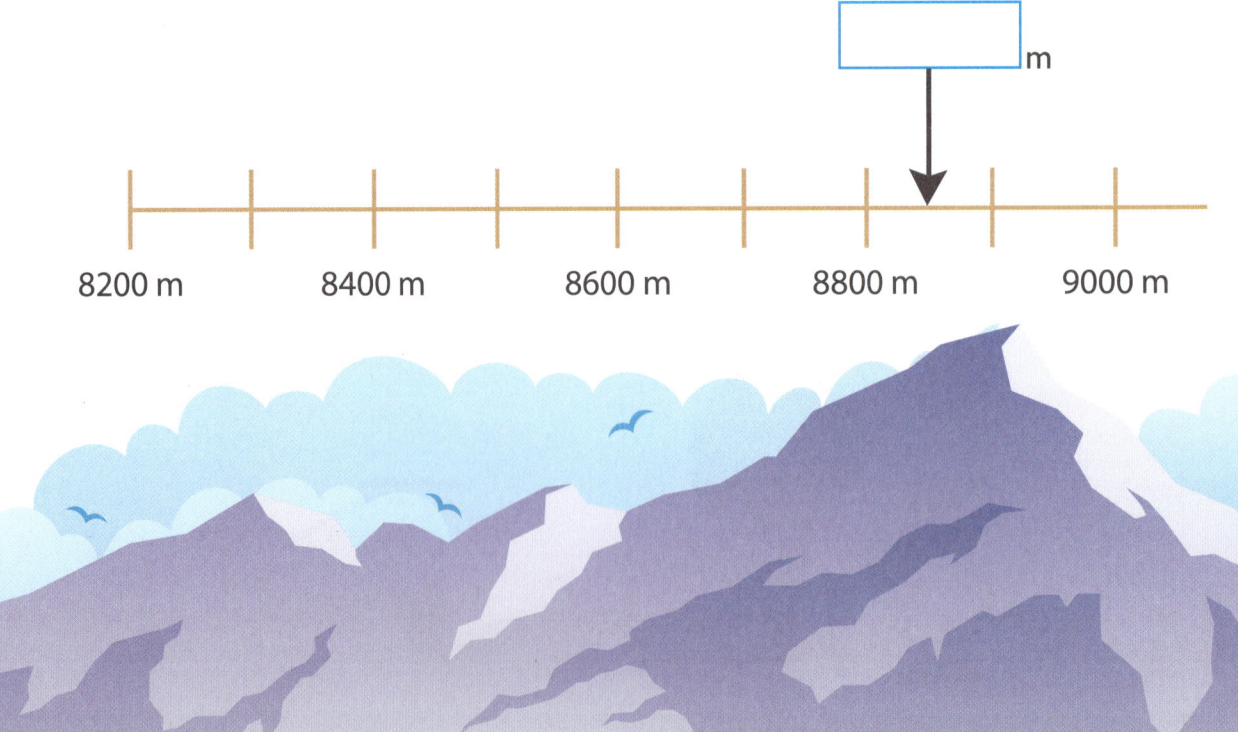

Your child needs to understand how to solve simple time problems and read the 24-hour clock. Practise counting around an analogue clock twice to show how one day is made up of 24 hours. Label the analogue clock 13:00, 14:00, 15:00, 16:00, etc.

6 The bar chart shows the estimated population in the UK in 2050.

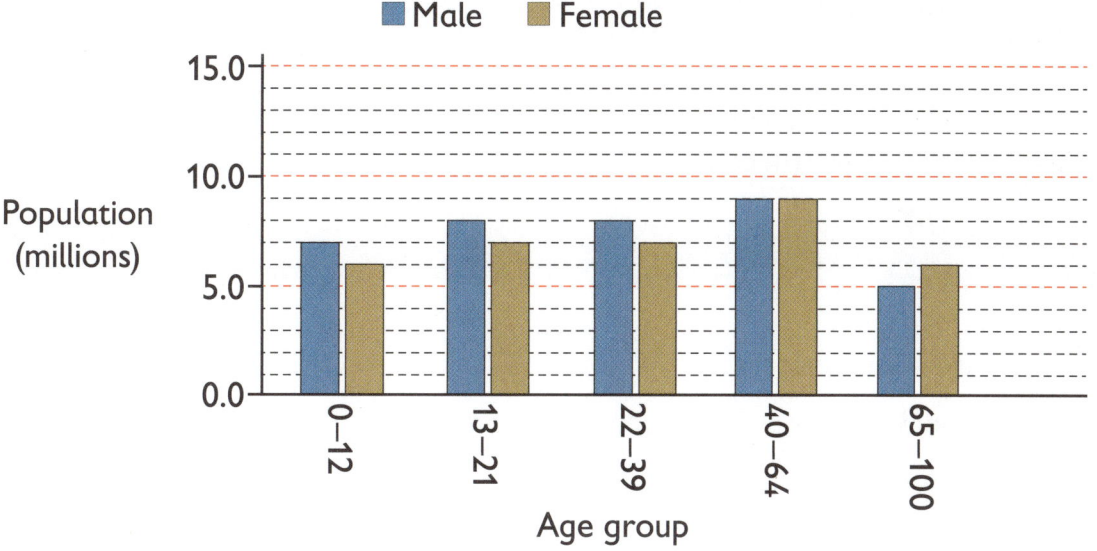

Using the information in the bar chart, tick to show whether each statement is **true** or **false**.

	True	False
The estimated male population at age 65–100 is 5 million.	☐	☐
The estimated female population at age 0–12 is 6 million.	☐	☐
The estimated male population at age 40–64 is double the estimated male population at age 65–100.	☐	☐
The estimated female population is 34 million.	☐	☐
The estimated total population is 72 million.	☐	☐

Dexter says, 'There is a difference of 1 million between the estimated population at age 0–12 and the estimated population at age 65–100.'

Do you agree? Explain your answer.

_____

_____

_____

_____

_____

_____

At the post office

At the post office, you can weigh parcels, look at the different shapes of parcels and buy stamps to post letters.

1 Here are some parcels.

Write the 3-D shape name for each parcel.

_____   _____   _____

2 Write the mass of each parcel.

A 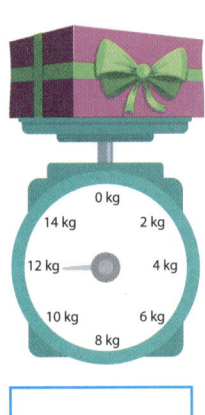   **B**    **C**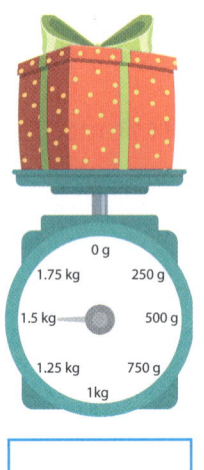

[_____] kg   [_____] kg   [_____] kg

The parcels are labelled 'small' or 'large' according to their mass (weight).

A small parcel has a mass up to 2 kg. A large parcel has a mass from 2.1 to 20 kg.

Label each of the parcels 'small' or 'large'.

A = _____   B = _____   C = _____

3) Different items are being posted.

Draw lines to match each item to its estimated mass.

| 500 g | 180 g | 2 kg | 30 g |

4) Here are some parcels to be posted.

A  **B**  **C**

☐   ☐   ☐

Tick the **heaviest** parcel.

Circle the **lightest** parcel.

Which **two** parcels add up to 3500 g together?

☐ and ☐

Calculate the difference between parcel B and parcel C. ☐ g

Your child needs to understand how to convert between different measures: grams to kilograms, millilitres to litres and centimetres to metres. They need to remember these key facts to help them solve conversion problems:
- **1 kg = 1000 g**
- **1 l = 1000 ml**
- **1 m = 100 cm**

5 The tables show the cost of posting small letters and large letters using a first class stamp or a second class stamp.

First class stamp	Cost
Small letter	£1.70
Large letter	£3.15

Second class stamp	Cost
Small letter	87p
Large letter	£1.55

How much does it cost to post two small letters using first class stamps? £ ☐

How much does it cost to post three small letters using second class stamps? £ ☐

How much does it cost to post one large letter using a first class stamp and one small letter using a second class stamp? £ ☐

You buy a first class stamp for a large letter and two second class stamps for small letters.
You pay for the stamps with a £10 note.
How much change do you get? £ ☐

6 A letter with a first class stamp is delivered within 1–2 days. A letter with a second class stamp is delivered within 3–4 days.

Use the calendar to answer the questions.

You post a letter using a second class stamp on Monday 15 February.

What is the **earliest** date the letter will be delivered?

_____

You post a letter with a first class stamp on Wednesday 24 February.

What is the **latest** date the letter will be delivered?

_____

7 Letters are put into post bags to take to the sorting office.

Round each post bag to the nearest **10**

Round each post bag to the nearest **100**

8 Stamps can be bought individually or in books.

How much money do you save if you buy a book of 6 stamps instead of 6 individual stamps?

1 individual stamp	87p
Book of 6 stamps	£5

☐ p

> Your child needs to understand how to round numbers to the nearest 10, 100 and 1000. They need to understand that when rounding to the nearest 100, if the value of the tens digit is 5 or more then round up to the next hundred; if it is 4 tens or less, round down.

At the garden centre

The garden centre has a team of gardeners who grow and sell plants, and measure and design gardens.

1 Seedlings are sold in trays. The cost per tray is £3.50

Rima wants to buy 100 seedling plants.

How many trays does Rima need to buy?

How much does Rima spend on the seedling plants? £

Zara spends £10.50 on trays of seedlings.
How many trays does she buy?

2 Compost is sold in bags.

Use the symbols < or > to compare the sizes of the bags.

3 Tim the gardener needs to calculate how much new fencing is needed for the perimeter of each garden.

Calculate the perimeter of each garden.

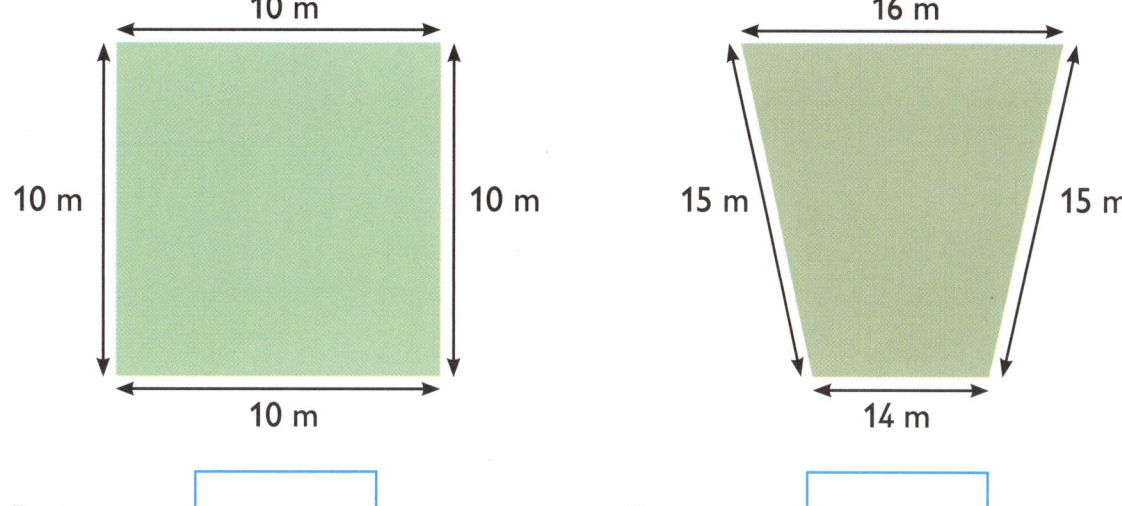

Perimeter = ☐ m   Perimeter = ☐ m

4 Fencing is sold in panels. The width of one fencing panel is 2 m.

How many panels of fencing does Tim need for the perimeter of each of these gardens?

Work out the perimeter first.

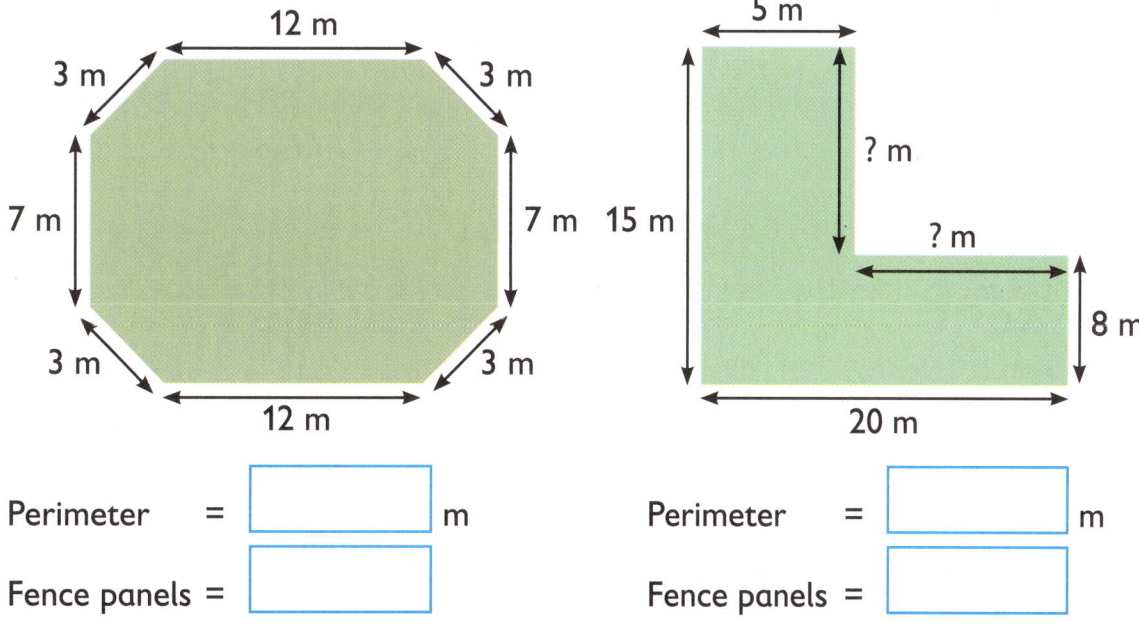

Perimeter = ☐ m   Perimeter = ☐ m

Fence panels = ☐   Fence panels = ☐

Perimeter is the total distance around a 2-D shape. Your child needs to be able to add up the length of each side to find the perimeter of a shape.

5 The garden centre uses water butts to collect rainwater for watering the plants.

Write the amount of water (in litres) in each water butt.

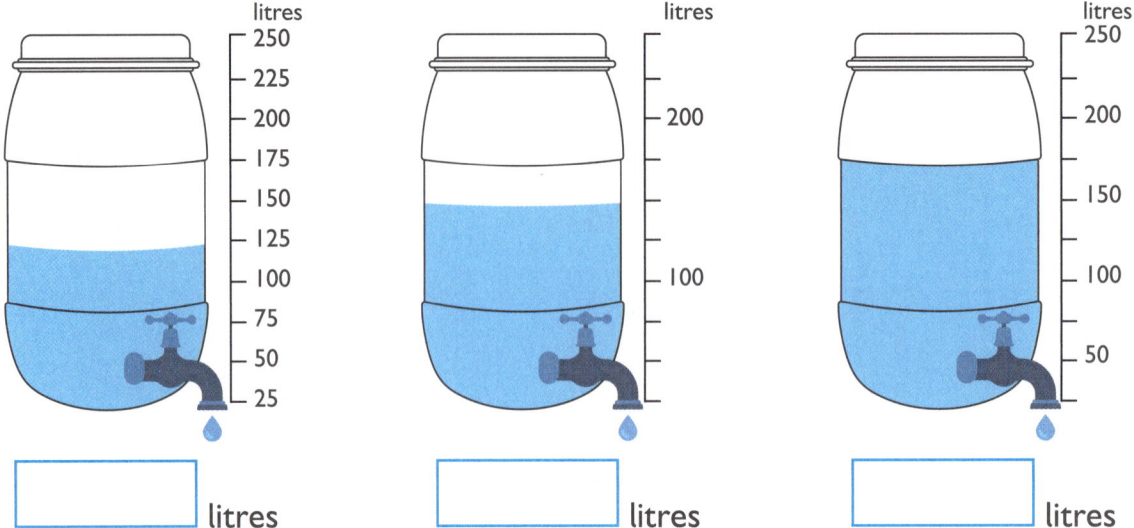

☐ litres   ☐ litres   ☐ litres

6 A new lawn is needed to cover this area in Anna's garden. Each square is 1 m.

Calculate the area of this shape.

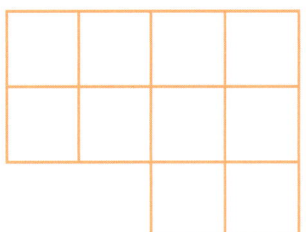

Area = ☐ m²

The cost of lawn is £8.50 per square metre.

How much does the new lawn cost?   £ ☐

Lawn is sold in 1.5 m rolls.

How many rolls of lawn are needed to cover the area?   ☐

Your child needs to understand how to find the area (the amount of space) taken up by a 2-D shape. Count the number of squares to work out the area of a shape.

7 The time graph shows the growth of a sunflower seed into a plant.

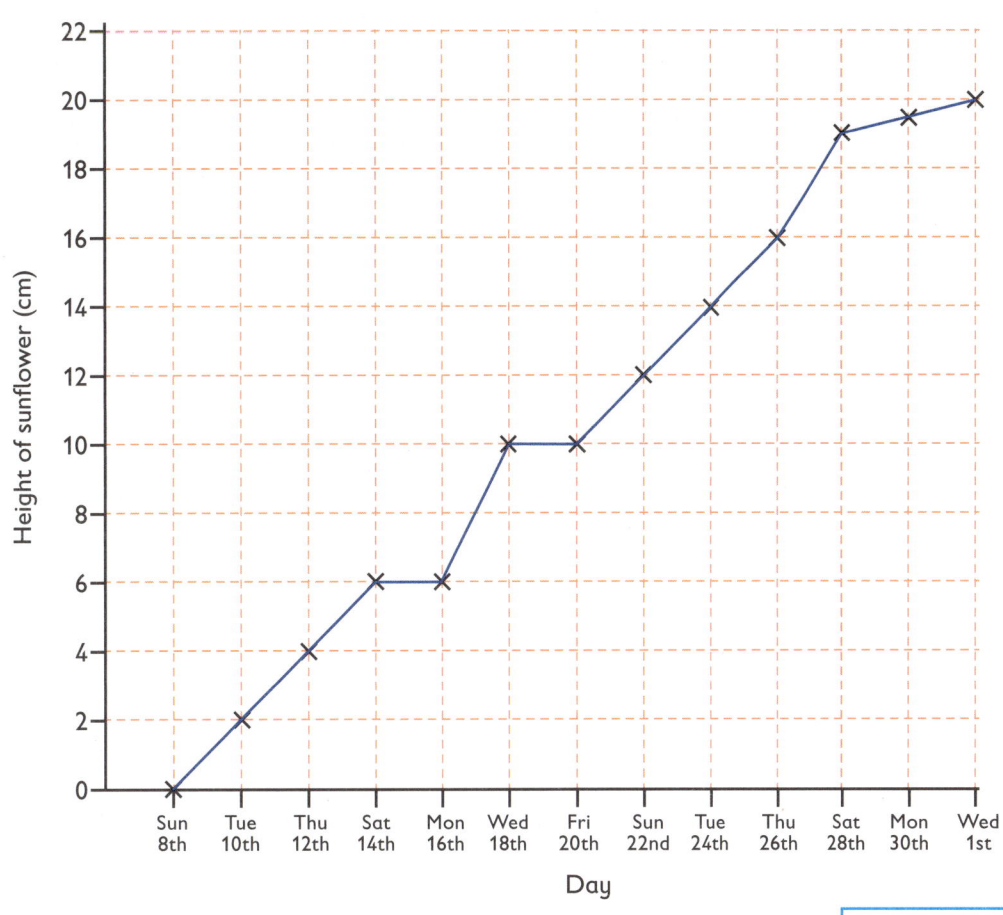

What is the height of the sunflower on Sunday 8th? ☐ cm

How much does the sunflower grow from Sunday 8th to Saturday 14th? ☐ cm

On what date is the height of the sunflower 14 cm? _____

How much does the sunflower grow from Saturday 28th to Wednesday 1st? ☐ cm

Omar says, 'The sunflower grew 10 cm between Monday 16th and Thursday 26th.'

Do you agree? Explain your answer.

_____

_____

_____

_____

Bake off!

Today we are making, selling and buying baked treats. When baking you need to find quantities and fractions of amounts and be able to measure ingredients.

1 Cat's Café sells slices of fruit pie.

Complete the calculations to show how much of each pie is left.

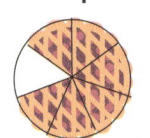 − $\boxed{\dfrac{2}{7}}$ = $\boxed{\dfrac{}{}}$

 − $\boxed{\dfrac{3}{8}}$ = $\boxed{\dfrac{}{}}$

 − $\boxed{\dfrac{4}{6}}$ = $\boxed{\dfrac{}{}}$

2 Cat has baked some muffins to sell in her cafe.

$\dfrac{1}{10}$ of the muffins are blueberry.

$\dfrac{3}{10}$ of the muffins are lemon.

18 of the muffins are chocolate.

Use the bar model to help you.

How many muffins are blueberry?

How many muffins are lemon?

How many muffins were baked in total?

Your child needs to understand how to add and subtract within one whole. When adding and subtracting fractions, the denominator (the bottom number) does not change. Try cutting an object (e.g. an orange) into 4 or 6 equal parts and practise taking away parts.

3 Jess has these ingredients to bake a chocolate birthday cake:

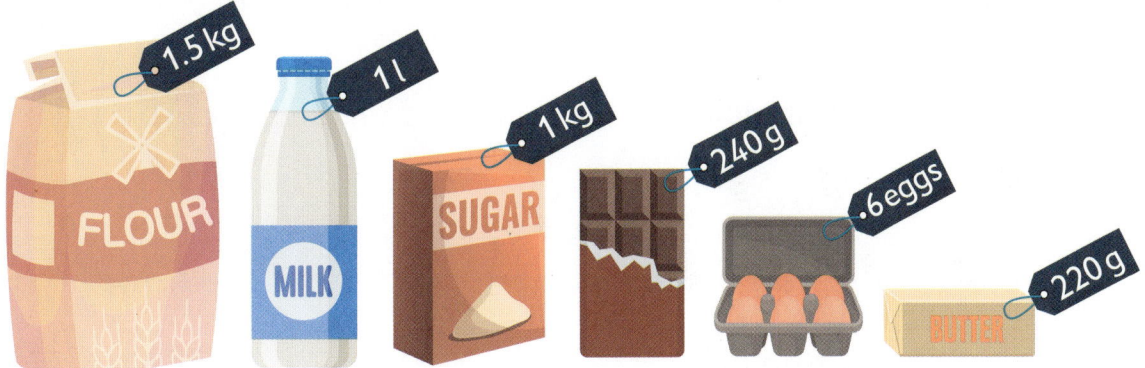

What quantity of each ingredient does Jess need?

$\frac{6}{10}$ of butter = ☐ g $\frac{1}{4}$ of sugar = ☐ g

$\frac{1}{5}$ of flour = ☐ g $\frac{1}{3}$ of eggs = ☐

$\frac{5}{8}$ of chocolate = ☐ g $\frac{2}{10}$ of milk = ☐ ml

4 Jess bakes the cake for 1 hour 30 minutes. She puts the cake in the oven at 5 minutes to midday.

On the clock, show the time she takes the cake out of the oven.

To find a fraction of a quantity, divide the quantity by the denominator (the bottom number) and then multiply the result by the numerator (the top number).
For example, $\frac{3}{5}$ of 250 is 250 ÷ 5 = 50, then 50 × 3 = 150

5 Bobby and Beth bake some flapjacks.
The pictograms show the amount of honey in the flapjacks.

Beth's flapjacks	
🐝🐝🐝🐝 🐝🐝🐝🐝	🐝 = 25 g
Bobby's flapjacks	
🐝🐝🐝🐝 🐝	🐝 = 50 g

How much honey is in Bobby's flapjacks? ☐ g

How much honey is in Beth's flapjacks? ☐ g

A jar of honey contains 227 grams.

How many jars of honey does Bobby need? ☐

How many jars of honey does Beth need? ☐

6 Bobby and Beth put their flapjacks into boxes.

Bobby has baked **24** flapjacks.
How many boxes will he need if he puts:

3 flapjacks in each box? ☐

4 flapjacks in each box? ☐

Beth has baked **36** flapjacks.
How many boxes will she need if she puts:

4 flapjacks in each box? ☐

6 flapjacks in each box? ☐

7 Rayan is buying ingredients to bake a cake. He uses this recipe:

Recipe
150 g of butter
3 eggs
250 g of flour
150 g of sugar
150 g of icing sugar
2 tubs of cream

Cost of ingredients	
100 g of butter	50p
1 egg	30p
50 g of flour	40p
75 g of sugar	60p
150 g of icing sugar	60p
1 tub of cream	50p

Rayan buys the amount he needs of some of the ingredients.

Write the cost of each of these ingredients.

Butter: £ ☐   Eggs: £ ☐   Sugar: £ ☐

Rayan pays using a £10 note. How much change will he get?   £ ☐

8 Katie stores some baked goods in her fridge-freezer.

6°C — Cake
3°C — Brownies
-3°C — Dough
-15°C — Muffins

What is the difference in temperature of where cake is stored and where dough is stored?

☐ °C

What is the difference in temperature of where brownies are stored and where muffins are stored?

☐ °C

Looking after the planet

Today we are thinking about how we can recycle, reduce and reuse to help look after our planet. We can look at percentages, costs and savings and weights of recycled items.

1 Recycling **1** plastic bottle saves enough energy to turn on a 60-watt lightbulb for 3 hours. Use this fact to complete the statements.

2 plastic bottles saves enough energy to turn on the lightbulb for

☐ hours.

5 plastic bottles saves enough energy to turn on the lightbulb for

☐ hours.

7 plastic bottles saves enough energy to turn on the lightbulb for

☐ hours.

2 The diagram shows what happens to waste plastic.

9% of plastic is recycled

? % of plastic is burned

79% of plastic is in landfill

How much more plastic is put in landfill than is recycled? ☐ %

How much plastic is burned? ☐ %

How much more plastic is put in landfill than is burned? ☐ %

Your child needs to understand that *per cent* relates to 'number of parts per hundred' so that they can work out the missing percentage or 'out of 100'. Practise calculating missing percentages with your child. For example, if 60% of children got a question right, what percentage of children got it wrong?

24

3 At Cat's Café, the cost of a regular coffee is £2.30

If a customer brings in their own cup, the cost is £1.80

How much do customers save if they bring in their own cup? [ ] p

How many cups of coffee do customers need to buy to save £5? [ ]

4 Ruben earns 50p per kilogram of aluminium cans that he collects and recycles.

80 aluminium cans are equal to 1 kilogram.

The pictogram shows the number of aluminium cans collected by Ruben's school to raise money for charity.

= 80 cans   Aluminium cans collected by school

How many kilograms of cans were collected by the school? [ ] kg

How much money did the school raise for charity? £ [ ]

How many more kilograms of cans does the school need to collect to raise £20? [ ] kg

Visiting a castle

Today we are visiting a castle and learning about its history. We can look at Roman numerals, weights and patterns of armour and coordinates of parts of the castle.

1 There is a clock in the entrance of the castle. The Roman numerals on the clock face are missing.

Write the Roman numerals on the clock face.

2 Engravings of Roman numerals can be seen around the castle.

Write the Roman numerals shown here in numbers.

XXIV = ☐   XCII = ☐   XLII = ☐

XVI = ☐   XIX = ☐   XXXVIII = ☐

LXXXIII = ☐   XLV = ☐   LIX = ☐

Your child needs to be able to read Roman numerals to 100 (I to C) and know that over time, the numeral system changed to include the concept of 0 and place value. Encourage your child to learn the value of the key Roman numerals: I = 1, V = 5, X = 10, L = 50, C = 100

3 Lily is interested in the armour exhibition and how heavy the knights' armour was.

Knight	Mass of armour
Sir Phoenix	26 kg
Sir Gawin	22 kg
Sir Tristan	25 kg
Sir Henry	23 kg
Sir Lancelot	24 kg

Lily rounds the weight (mass) of each knight's armour to the nearest 10 and adds them all up.

She says, 'The total mass of all the knights' armour rounded to the nearest 10 is 120 kg.'

Do you agree? Explain your reason.

_____

_____

4 A knight would always carry a shield.

Complete the shield so that it has a symmetrical pattern.

5 The grid shows a plan of the castle.

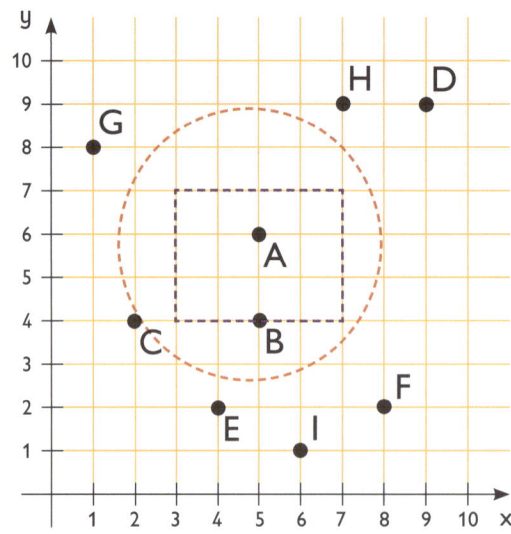

Write the coordinates for each of these parts of the castle.

Main castle (A) ☐

Drawbridge (B) ☐

Moat (C) ☐

Bailey (D) ☐

Flower garden (E) ☐

Pond (F) ☐

Jousting (G) ☐

Herb garden (H) ☐

Oak tree (I) ☐

The keep is not shown on the plan of the castle. It is 3 right and 4 up from the coordinates point of the bailey.

What are the coordinates of the keep? ☐

Your child needs to be able to read and describe positions on a coordinates grid. To find the coordinates of a point, read along the x-axis (horizontal) first and then the y-axis (vertical).

6 The castle has 540 windows. $\frac{3}{5}$ of the windows are stained glass.

How many windows are **not** stained glass?

The castle has two turrets: one turret is 2900 cm high and the other is 3400 cm high.

What is the difference in height between the two turrets? ☐ cm

The castle has 12 stables. Each stable has 9 horses.

How many horses in total are kept at the castle?

The castle has a banquet hall.

The banquet table is 5 m long and 2 m wide.

What is the perimeter of the banquet table? ☐ m

7 After your visit to the castle, you make a model of the castle using 3-D shapes.

Write how many of each 3-D shape are used to make the model.

Cube ☐

Pyramid ☐

Cylinder ☐

At the leisure centre

You want to join your local leisure centre. You are looking at information about classes and activities on timetables and working out the different options and costs for membership.

This is a timetable of classes on Saturday mornings at the leisure centre.

	Pool	Gym	Studio	Courts
Session 1 6.05 am–7.00 am	Aqua fit			
Session 2 7.05 am–8.00 am	Lane swimming	Power gym	Dance fitness	Tennis level 3
Session 3 8.05 am–9.00 am	Aqua fit	Power gym	Junior dance	
Session 4 9.05 am–10.00 am	Lane swimming	Junior gym	Dance fitness	Tennis level 1
Session 5 10.05 am–11.00 am	Aqua fit		Yoga	Tennis level 2
Session 6 11.05 am–12.00 pm	Family swim		Dance fitness	

This is a table showing the cost of membership at the leisure centre.

Membership type	Included	Cost
Standard	Gym only	£29 per month
Silver	Gym + swim	Standard + £7 per month
Gold	Gym + swim + studio	Standard + £12 per month
Platinum	Everything included	Gold + £7.50 per month

1. Use the information in the timetable of classes on page 30 to answer these questions.

What time does the first dance fitness class start? ☐

What time does tennis level 2 start? ☐

How many aqua fit sessions are there? ☐

Where does yoga take place? _____

How many minutes does each class last? ☐

How many junior classes are there? ☐

What time does the earliest class start? _____

Stanley says, 'Dance fitness is the most commonly occurring class on the timetable.'

Do you agree? Explain your answer.

_____

_____

2. Use the information in the membership table on page 30 to answer these questions.

How much does standard membership cost per month? £ ☐

How much does silver membership cost per month? £ ☐

How much would gold membership cost for 2 months? £ ☐

What is the difference in cost between gold membership and platinum membership? £ ☐

Mai says, 'Platinum membership costs approximately £20 more than standard membership.'
Do you agree? Explain your answer.

_____

_____

> Your child needs to be able to read tables and timetables. Explain that it is important to look at the labels at the top of each column and on the left of each row to understand the information shown. Practise reading timetables together, such as bus and train timetables.

Answers

Pages 4–7

1. £4.59, 59p; £6.85, 85p; £5.49, 49p
2. 1500 g, 2300 g, 750 g; £1.35; 90p
3. Free circled; £1.10 circled; Free circled
4. 930 points, 122 points, 150 points
5. £10.25; £21.30; £43.90
6. 150; 150; 500
7. 9000; 3500

Pages 8–11

1. Mississippi, Congo, Amazon, Nile; 2884 km; 6300 km
2.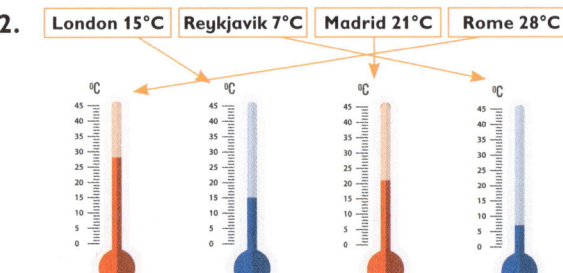
3. €1.20; €2.40; €3.60; €4.80; €6; €7.20; €13.20
4. 05:30; 12:30; 18:30; 15:00; 03:30; 22:30
5. 8850 m
6. True; True; False; False; True
   No. The estimated population at age 0–12 is 13 million and the estimated population at age 65–100 is 11 million, so the difference is 2 million.

Pages 12–15

1. cube; cuboid; cylinder
2. 12 kg, 9 kg, 1.5 kg; A = large, B = large, C = small
3. 500 g – trainers; 180 g – phone; 2 kg – books; 30 g – letter
4. C ticked; B circled; A and C; 1250 g
5. £3.40; £2.61; £4.02; £5.11
6. Thursday 18th February; Friday 26th February
7. 750, 390, 500; 500, 800, 600
8. 22p

Pages 16–19

1. 4; £14; 3
2. 80 l > 75 l; 45 l > 38 l; 40 l < 60 l; 72 l > 55 l
3. 40 m; 60 m
4. A: Perimeter = 50 m, Fence panels = 25
   B: Perimeter = 70 m, Fence panels = 35
5. 125 litres; 150 litres; 175 litres
6. 10 m²; £85; 7
7. 0 cm; 6 cm; Tuesday 24th; 1 cm
   Yes. On Monday 16th the sunflower was 6 cm and on Thursday 26th it was 16 cm. So, it grew 10 cm.

Pages 20–23

1. $\frac{4}{7}$; $\frac{3}{8}$; $\frac{2}{6}$
2. 3; 9; 30
3. 132 g butter; 250 g sugar; 300 g flour; 2 eggs; 150 g chocolate; 200 ml milk
4.
5. 250 g; 200 g; 2 jars; 1 jar
6. 8, 6; 9, 6
7. Butter: £0.75, Eggs: £0.90, Sugar: £1.20; £7.15
8. 9°C, 18°C

Pages 24–25

1. 6; 15; 21
2. 70%; 12%; 67%
3. 50p; 10
4. 30 kg; £15; 10 kg

Pages 26–29

1. Clockwise from the top: XII; I; II; III; IV; V; VI; VII; VIII; IX; X; XI
2. XXIV = 24; XCII = 92; XLII = 42; XVI = 16; XIX = 19; XXXVIII = 38; LXXXIII = 83; XLV = 45; LIX = 59
3. Yes. 30 kg + 20 kg + 30 kg + 20 kg + 20 kg gives a total of 120 kg, rounded to the nearest 10.
4. Symmetrical pattern drawn to match the pattern shown
5. Main castle (5,6); Drawbridge (5,4); Moat (2,4); Bailey (9,9); Flower garden (4,2); Pond (8,2); Jousting (1,8); Herb garden (7,9); Oak tree (6,1); Keep (12,13)
6. 216; 500 cm; 108; 14 m
7. Cube: 8; Pyramid: 3; Cylinder: 1

Pages 30–31

1. 7.05 am; 10.05 am; 3; Studio; 55 minutes; 2; 6:05 am
   No. There are 3 dance fitness classes, but there are also 3 aqua fit classes (and 3 tennis sessions).
2. £29; £36; £82; £7.50
   Yes. The difference in price is £19.50, which is £20 when rounded to the nearest whole pound.